Kids Cook Dinner

23 Healthy, Budget-Friendly Meals

from the best-selling Cooking Class series

Deanna F. Cook

Storey Publishing

The mission of Storey Publishing is to serve our customers by publishing practical information that encourages personal independence in harmony with the environment.

Edited by Deborah Balmuth and Lisa H. Hiley
Art direction and book design by Ash Austin
Text production by Jennifer Jepson Smith

Cover photography by © Carl Tremblay
Interior photography by © Carl Tremblay, 4, 7, 8, 9 ex. b.l., 10–13, 20–23, 28, 29, 34–41, 44–47, 50–57; © Julie Bidwell, 3, 18, 19, 24–27, 30–33, 42, 43, 48, 49, 58, 59 ex. 4 & 5, 60–63; Mars Vilaubi © Storey Publishing, LLC, 9 b.l., 59 4 & 5
Illustrations and graphics by Ash Austin © Storey Publishing, LLC

Storey books are available at special discounts when purchased in bulk for premiums and sales promotions as well as for fund-raising or educational use. Special editions or book excerpts can also be created to specification. For details, please call 800-827-8673, or send an email to sales@storey.com.

Storey Publishing
210 MASS MoCA Way
North Adams, MA 01247
storey.com

Printed in China by R.R. Donnelley
10 9 8 7 6 5 4 3 2 1

LIBRARY OF CONGRESS CATALOGING-IN-PUBLICATION DATA
Names: Cook, Deanna F., 1965– author.
Title: Kids cook dinner : 23 healthy, budget-friendly meals from the best-selling Cooking Class series / Deanna F. Cook.
Description: North Adams, MA : Storey Publishing, [2022] | Audience: Ages 8–12 | Audience: Grades 4–6
Identifiers: LCCN 2021059994 (print) | LCCN 2021059995 (ebook) | ISBN 9781635864632 (paperback) | ISBN 9781635864649 (ebook)
Subjects: LCSH: Cooking--Juvenile literature. | Quick and easy cooking--Juvenile literature. | LCGFT: Cookbooks.
Classification: LCC TX652.5 .C6354 2022 (print) | LCC TX652.5 (ebook) | DDC 641.5/123--dc23/eng/20211213
LC record available at https://lccn.loc.gov/2021059994
LC ebook record available at https://lccn.loc.gov/2021059995

Contents

Super Sliders

RECIPES

Let's Get Going

Tonight you're in charge of making dinner! In this cookbook made just for you, you'll discover some easy, tasty, and inexpensive recipes you can serve up any night of the week. You can make **Popcorn Chicken**, **Cheesy Bean Quesadillas**, **Nutty Noodles**, **Fried Rice**, and many other recipes with ingredients you may already have in your fridge—or affordable ingredients you can buy in the store—and your family will thank you!

Before you put on your apron, take a look at the introduction. Learn some cooking skills, like how to chop veggies or make a stir-fry. Review the kitchen safety guidelines. And check out the money-saving tips for grocery shopping, so your meals won't break the bank. Then pick one of these delicious dinner recipes and start cooking. You'll feel proud to say, **"Dinner's ready!"**

READ UP ON KITCHEN RULES

When you're ready to start cooking, follow these basic kitchen rules.
Be sure to ask for help, if you need it, in your cooking adventures.

1
Start by asking an adult for permission.
At first, have a grown-up cook with you if you are working over a hot stove, baking in an oven, or using a sharp knife.

2
Wash your hands
with warm water and soap before you handle food.

3
Roll up long sleeves and wear an apron.
Tie back long hair to keep it away from the food. Stand on a stool if you can't reach the counter or stove.

4
Read the recipe from start to finish before you begin.
Follow the recipe steps closely.

5
Put out all the ingredients you'll need
(see the recipe's "Here's What You Need" list) to be sure you have everything. If you are missing something, make a list and have a grown-up take you to the grocery store before you start your cooking project.

6

Wash all fruits and vegetables
before you start chopping and measuring. Use a separate cutting board for preparing meat, and always wash your hands and utensils with plenty of soap and hot water after handling meat.

7
Take out all the tools you'll need
for your recipe, from measuring cups to bowls.

8
Measure carefully
(see the tips on page 12).

9
Preheat.
Let the oven come to the correct temperature before you put in your pans or baking sheets. If you don't, your food will take longer to bake or will cook unevenly.

10

Use a timer.
But if the dish doesn't seem quite done when the timer goes off, let it cook for another 5 minutes or so.

11

Stay in the kitchen!
Never leave the room if you are cooking something on the stove or baking something in the oven.

12

Use pot holders for hot pans.
Always be careful handling pots, pans, and baking sheets that have been on a hot burner or in the oven.

13

Trust your sense of smell.
If you smell something burning, move your pan or pot off the hot stove and lower the heat (or turn it off altogether). If you're baking and smell food burning, turn off the oven and take out the food, even if the timer hasn't gone off yet.

14

Give your food a taste test.
If you'd like it to be more flavorful, add a little salt (which helps bring out flavor). Or add extra spice. Part of the fun and creativity in cooking is customizing flavors to match your personal tastes.

15

Remember to turn off the stove or oven
after you're done cooking.

16

Leave the kitchen sparkling clean!
Put away the ingredients, wipe down the countertops, and wash the dishes.

LESSON 2
DO YOUR KITCHEN PREP WORK

Many of the recipes in this book call for some prep work, such as grating carrots or crushing garlic, before you actually make the dish. Read the ingredients list to find out what you need to do. With all your prep work done in advance, you won't have to stop in the middle of cooking. Learn these prep skills and you'll be ready to make all the recipes.

Chop and dice: To cut vegetables and other foods into small pieces with a sharp knife (practice with a grown-up first). To **chop**, cut food into pieces about 1 inch square. To **dice**, cut the pieces about ½ inch square.

Mince: To cut herbs and other foods into tiny pieces using a sharp knife or clean kitchen scissors.

Juice: To squeeze the juice from a citrus fruit, like a lime or lemon, by cutting it in half and then pressing the halves on a juicer. Twist the fruit back and forth to get out all the juice.

Crush garlic: To mash raw garlic. You'll need a garlic press. Peel off the papery skin of one clove. Put it into the press and squeeze the press shut. The crushed garlic will ooze out of the end.

Grate: To rub a food, like cheese, a carrot, or ginger, against the sharp-edged holes of a grater to shred it. If the piece of food you're holding gets small, stop grating to protect your fingers.

Peel: To remove the skin from a fruit or vegetable by peeling it with a vegetable peeler. There are two kinds of peelers: straight peelers (shown) and Y-shaped peelers.

WASH LETTUCE & FRESH HERBS

1 Fill a salad spinner with cold water. Add the lettuce leaves or fresh herbs and swish them around with your hands. Let sit for at least 5 minutes. The dirt will sink to the bottom.

2 Lift the spinner basket out of the water. Drain the water. Put the basket of lettuce or herbs back in the empty spinner.

3 Put on the cover. Press the top (or turn the handle) to spin the basket around. The water will fly out, leaving the lettuce or herbs dry.

CHOP AN ONION

1 Cut the onion in half lengthwise. Lay the halves flat on a cutting board and cut off the ends. Peel off the skin.

2 Slice one onion half crosswise, cutting it into as many slices as you can. Hold the knife firmly and tuck your fingers back.

3 Flip the onion slices sideways, and lay them flat on the cutting board. Chop them into small pieces. Then finish off with a quick chop of all the pieces. Repeat steps 2 and 3 with the other half.

SHARPEN YOUR COOKING SKILLS

Read the recipe's directions carefully. Here are definitions of some key cooking terms you'll see in some of the steps. Check back here if you're not sure what to do in a recipe.

Stir: To mix ingredients with a spoon, whisk, or spatula. Don't use metal spoons or spatulas with nonstick pans.

Whisk: To combine ingredients with a whisk. You can whisk eggs and milk in a bowl or whisk sauces in a pan on the stovetop.

Bake or roast: To cook with dry heat in the oven in a sheet pan or open roasting pan. Be sure to preheat the oven to the temperature listed in the recipe.

Stir-fry: To cook food in a wok or skillet in oil over high heat.

Melt: To turn a solid into a liquid by applying heat. You can melt butter in a saucepan or skillet over low heat or in a bowl in a microwave. You can melt cheese in a grilled sandwich or on top of a pizza in the oven.

Sauté: To cook food lightly in a little oil in a hot skillet.

Toast: To brown lightly on both sides. You can do this on a griddle or in a toaster, an oven, or a toaster oven.

Boil: To heat liquid to a temperature high enough to cause bubbles to form and break rapidly on the surface. When boiling, always use a saucepan that is big enough to keep ingredients from boiling over the top.

Simmer: To cook liquid slowly over low heat. The bubbles rise to the surface much more slowly when liquid is simmering than when it's boiling.

HOW TO . . .
GRATE FRESH GINGER

Many Asian dishes, such as fried rice (page 36), are flavored with grated fresh ginger.

1 Peel the ginger with a vegetable peeler.

2 Rub the ginger against the side of a cheese grater to grate it. (To dice it, chop it into small cubes with a sharp knife.)

11

LESSON 4
MEASURE CAREFULLY

When following a recipe, it's important to measure the ingredients. Here are some tips for success.

Liquid ingredients. Measure larger amounts of milk, water, and other liquids in a glass or plastic liquid measuring cup. Pour the liquid into the cup, and read the measurements marked on the cup from eye level.

Dry ingredients. Measure flour, sugar, and other dry ingredients with dry measuring cups or measuring spoons that can be leveled off. Fill the cup or spoon with the ingredient, and then run the flat part of a butter knife across it to get an exact measure.

For smaller amounts, such as a teaspoon, use measuring spoons. Work over a small bowl to catch any spills.

Butter. Sticks of butter are usually wrapped in paper that's marked with tablespoon measurements. Find the line marking the amount of butter you need, and then carefully cut the stick there, slicing straight down through the paper. Unwrap the portion you need and add it to your recipe.

LESSON 5
KITCHEN SAFETY

Many of the recipes in this book require that you keep safety measures in mind, especially when you use sharp knives or a hot oven. Here are some rules for working in the kitchen without getting hurt.

Knives and graters. Make sure your knife is sharpened properly (a dull knife is more dangerous because you have to press down hard while you're cutting and the knife can easily slip) and hold it firmly, with your fingers out of the way of the blade. Always cut with the blade moving away from your hand.

When you use a grater, watch out that you don't accidentally scrape the tip of your finger or your knuckles. That can hurt a lot! Dry your hands before cutting and grating—wet hands are slippery!

Microwave. If you don't already know how to use your microwave, ask an adult to show you. Always use microwave-safe dishes. Glass, ceramic, some plastics, and paper towels are fine. Never use metal or aluminum foil in a microwave. They could damage the microwave or even cause a fire.

Oven, stovetop, and toaster oven. Before you turn on the stove or oven, have an adult show you the proper way to use it and explain the different settings. When you are cooking something on the stove, always stay in the kitchen!

When you open a hot oven, turn your face away to avoid the blast of heat that will rise up out of it. Always use oven mitts when handling hot pans and baking trays.

When you're cooking on a stovetop, turn the handle of your pan to the side so you don't accidentally knock it off the stove. Be sure to turn off the stovetop or oven when you have finished cooking.

EQUIVALENTS & CONVERSIONS

Here's a handy chart to help you convert recipe measurements.

- **1 teaspoon** = 5 milliliters
- **1 tablespoon** = 3 teaspoons = ½ fluid ounce = 45 milliliters
- **¼ cup** = 4 tablespoons = 60 milliliters
- **½ cup** = 4 fluid ounces = 120 milliliters
- **1 cup** = 8 fluid ounces = 240 milliliters
- **1 pint** = 2 cups = 16 fluid ounces = 480 milliliters
- **1 quart** = 2 pints = 4 cups = 0.95 liter

Money-Saving Tips for Grocery Shopping

When you go to the grocery store, you can save money (and sharpen your math skills!) by following these tips. (See page 64 for an example of a meal-planning checklist.)

Start with a meal plan. Before you head to the store, jot down some dinners you love. Write a meal plan for the week. That way, you won't be tempted to buy extra ingredients you don't plan to eat and you'll cut back on food waste.

Make a grocery list. Look at the ingredients that you need for each dinner recipe. Check to see if you have the ingredients in your fridge or cupboards already. If you don't, put those items on the grocery list.

Look for coupons and sales. Have your family sign up for your local grocery store emails so you get store rewards and coupons. You can plan dinners around what's on sale. For instance, if this week's flyer shows that chicken is on sale, add a chicken-based recipe to your meal plan. Use coupons to buy items that you need or to stock up for future menus.

Compare unit prices. When you get to the grocery store, look for the unit price stickers (not the price tag) for each item. Comparing unit prices will help you determine the best bargain. It's an easier way to figure out which item costs less than looking at the price tag.

Buy in bulk. It is usually less expensive to buy bulk packages of food when they are on sale, especially for foods you eat a lot. You can also buy staples like rice and beans in the bulk or dry bin section of your store, and they are often less expensive than packaged versions.

Be careful not to buy too much of something you don't often use, though. A 5-pound jar of mayonnaise might go bad before you finish it up.

Go generic. Think about buying the store brand or the generic brand of the foods you like. The store brand is often the exact same product in a different package at a lower price.

CALCULATE THE COST

It's pretty simple to figure out how much a meal costs to make. Just add the prices of all the ingredients and divide that total by the number of servings to find the cost per serving.

You don't need to include small amounts of staple ingredients, like a tablespoon of butter or a teaspoon of salt, in your prices.

Here's an example:

Cheesy Bean Quesadillas

1 package of
6 flour tortillas $2.39
                          +
1 package of
grated cheese $1.99
                          +
1 can of
black beans $0.59

Total: $4.97

$4.97 ÷ 6 servings

$0.83 per serving!

LOOK AT YOUR PLATE

When you are planning meals, try to balance the types of healthy food you serve. Here's a good way to think about it.

Most of your calories should come from fresh or frozen fruits and vegetables and whole grains. You also need protein from seafood, meat, beans, nuts, or soy products. And you need calcium from milk, yogurt, cheese, or fortified milk alternatives.

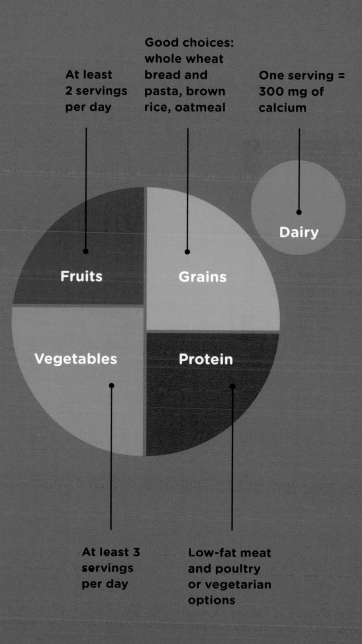

At least 2 servings per day

Good choices: whole wheat bread and pasta, brown rice, oatmeal

One serving = 300 mg of calcium

Dairy

Fruits

Grains

Vegetables

Protein

At least 3 servings per day

Low-fat meat and poultry or vegetarian options

What Does a Nutritional Label Tell You?

All packaged foods have labels that outline the nutritional content. Here's how to read them to find out if a food is good for you.

> **Ingredients: Tomato Puree (Water, Tomato Paste), Extra-Virgin Olive Oil, Sea Salt, Dehydrated Onion, Onion Powder, Citric Acid, Oregano, Basil, Black Pepper, Garlic Powder**

Ingredients list. The ingredients are listed in order with the largest amount first. If you see sugar at the beginning of the list, it means that food has lots of sugar. In this label for spaghetti sauce, tomato puree is listed first, which tells you there is more of it than any other ingredient.

Look for ingredients on the list that are familiar whole foods, like tomatoes or wheat, and try to choose foods with ingredients you can pronounce. Some additives, like citric acid, are necessary to help food last longer, but foods with lots of ingredients that sound like chemicals aren't the best choice.

Nutrition Facts

8 servings per container

Serving size 2/3 cup (55g)

Amount per serving

Calories 230

% Daily Value*

Total Fat 8g	**10%**
Saturated Fat 1g	**5%**
Trans Fat 0g	
Cholesterol 0mg	**0%**
Sodium 160mg	**7%**
Total Carbohydrate 37g	**13%**
Dietary Fiber 4g	**14%**
Total Sugars 12g	
Includes 10g Added Sugars	**20%**
Protein 3g	
Vitamin D 2mcg	10%
Calcium 260mg	20%
Iron 8mg	45%
Potassium 235mg	6%

* The % Daily Value (DV) tells you how much a nutrient in a serving of food contributes to a daily diet. 2,000 calories a day is used for general nutrition advice.

Serving size. This tells you how many calories and how many grams of fat, fiber, and other nutrients are in a single serving. Keep in mind that the serving size can be much smaller than the amount you might actually eat.

Calories. Your body needs healthy sources of calories to grow and be strong. This number shows the amount of energy you will get from eating one serving of this food.

Total fat. Some fats, such as those in olive oil, are good for us, but avoid trans fats as much as you can. Trans fats are found in many prepared foods but they aren't as good for you.

Sugar. Many foods have added sugar, often in the form of corn syrup. Natural sugar is what you find in bananas or orange juice. As much as possible, choose foods that don't have any added sugar.

Other nutrients. Nutrition labels also tell you the amount of protein, fiber, and other nutrients, such as iron, vitamin D, and calcium, a food has. As a rule of thumb, foods with more fiber and more protein provide more fuel for your body.

Cheesy Bean Quesadillas

MAKES 4 QUESADILLAS

For a **quick school-night supper**, cook a batch of these cheesy quesadillas. Serve them with cooked corn (see page 25) and **salsa on the side**.

(see page 25)

HERE'S WHAT YOU NEED

- 8 flour tortillas
- 1 (15.5-ounce) can refried beans
- 1½ cups shredded Monterey Jack cheese
- 1½ teaspoons butter

HERE'S WHAT YOU DO

1 Place a tortilla on a plate or cutting board. Add a few spoonfuls of refried beans, and spread them out with the back of the spoon. Sprinkle evenly with some of the grated cheese. Place a second tortilla on top.

2 Melt the butter in a skillet or griddle over medium heat. Place one or two quesadillas in the skillet. Cook until the cheese begins to melt and the bottom tortilla is light brown, 2 or 3 minutes.

3 Flip and cook on the other side until light brown. Remove the quesadilla(s) from the pan, and place on a cutting board. Repeat with the rest of the ingredients to make more quesadillas.

4 Use a pizza cutter or a knife to cut each quesadilla into wedges.

5 Arrange the wedges on a plate and serve with salsa.

Hearty Grilled Cheese

MAKES 2 SANDWICHES

These tasty sandwiches are like **French toast filled with ham and melted cheese**. They make a quick and filling dinner. Serve with carrot sticks or a salad on the side (see page 22).

(see page 22)

HERE'S WHAT YOU NEED

- 4 slices bread
- 4 slices ham
- 4 slices cheese (American, Swiss, or cheddar cheese, or any kind)
- Mustard (optional)
- 1 egg
- 3 tablespoons milk
- Pinch of salt
- ¾ tablespoon butter

For a shortcut, you can skip the egg dip.

HERE'S WHAT YOU DO

1

Make two simple ham-and-cheese sandwiches, spreading one slice of bread for each sandwich with mustard, if you'd like.

2

Whisk the egg, milk, and salt together in a shallow bowl.

3

Melt the butter in a frying pan or an electric skillet over medium-high heat. Dip one side of one sandwich in the egg batter, then dip the other side and place in the hot pan.

4

Dip both sides of the second sandwich in the egg batter, and set it in the pan next to the first one. Cook the sandwiches on the first side until golden brown, about 3 minutes.

5

Flip the sandwiches with a spatula. Cook on the second side for another 3 minutes.

6

Using the spatula, move the sandwiches from the pan to a plate, slice them in half, and serve.

Supper Side Salad

MAKES 4 TO 6 SERVINGS

Add a fresh, tasty side dish of salad to dinner! This recipe uses Greek salad **favorites like feta, tomato, and olives**, but you can make a side salad with any veggies you have on hand. **Mix up the dressing** and store leftovers in the fridge.

HERE'S WHAT YOU NEED

DRESSING
- ½ cup olive oil
- ¼ cup lemon juice (about 1 lemon)
- 1 garlic clove, crushed
- 1 teaspoon dried oregano
- ½ teaspoon salt
- ¼ teaspoon ground black pepper

SALAD
- 1 head romaine lettuce, chopped
- 1 large tomato, cut into wedges
- 1 small cucumber, cut into half rounds
- 1 small red onion, sliced
- ½ cup kalamata olives, pitted
- ½ cup crumbled feta cheese

HERE'S WHAT YOU DO

1

To make the dressing, pour the oil into a glass jar with tight-fitting lid.

2

Add the lemon juice, garlic, oregano, salt, and pepper.

3

Cover the jar with the lid, closing it tightly. Shake it up and set aside.

4

Place the lettuce, tomato, cucumber, and onion in a large salad bowl.

5

Top with the olives and crumbled feta cheese.

6

Drizzle the dressing over the salad. Toss with salad tongs.

Roasted Roots

MAKES 4 TO 6 SERVINGS

For a healthy side dish, try roasting up some vegetables. This is one of the **easiest ways to cook veggies**, and it makes them **extra delicious**.

You can roast just about any kind of vegetable. This recipe calls for root veggies, which are potatoes and beets and other vegetables that grow underground. Add or subtract vegetables from the ingredient list as you like.

TIP For **homemade tater tots**, cook just the potatoes and garlic.

HERE'S WHAT YOU NEED

- 4 medium potatoes
- 2 medium beets
- 2 green bell peppers
- 1 medium onion
- 3 garlic cloves
- 2–3 tablespoons olive oil
- 1 teaspoon salt

Preheat the oven to 425°F (220°C).

HERE'S WHAT YOU DO

1 Peel the potatoes and beets. Cut the potatoes, beets, green bell peppers, and onion into 1-inch chunks. Thinly slice the garlic.

2 Place all the veggies on a large baking sheet. Drizzle with the olive oil and sprinkle with the salt.

3 Toss with your (clean!) hands. Arrange the veggies in a single layer. Roast for about 45 minutes, until lightly browned and soft inside. Stir them every 15 minutes or so with tongs or a spatula.

HOW TO . . .

COOK FROZEN VEGETABLES

You've heard it before—it's important to eat your veggies! They have nutrients that help you grow strong and keep you healthy. An inexpensive (and easy!) way to get your veggies is to cook frozen vegetables. Frozen veggies are just as healthy as fresh ones and are sometimes easier to find at the store. A few favorites are corn, peas, spinach, broccoli, green beans, and shelled edamame. Or try mixed vegetables!

STOVETOP METHOD

1 Bring 1 cup of water to boil in a medium pot over high heat.

2 Carefully add the vegetables to the pot, being careful not to splash hot water.

3 Turn the heat to low and cook until the veggies are tender, 4 to 6 minutes. (You can also check the recommended cooking time on the package.)

4 Set a colander in your sink and drain the cooked veggies in it. Or use a slotted spoon to scoop the veggies out of the hot water and directly onto dinner plates.

MICROWAVE METHOD

1 Pour 1 cup of the vegetables into a microwave-safe bowl.

2 Add about ¼ cup of water.

3 Heat on high for 2 minutes. Check for doneness. Stir the veggies, cook for another minute, and check again. Keep cooking and checking until the veggies are cooked the way you like them.

4 Set a colander in your sink, and drain the cooked veggies in it. Or use a slotted spoon to scoop the veggies out of the hot water and directly onto dinner plates.

Corn & Black Bean Salad

MAKES 6 TO 8 SERVINGS

This recipe has loads of corn, tomatoes, and other veggies. Serve the salad with tortilla chips on the side. Or wrap it up in a tortilla to make a quick and easy burrito.

HERE'S WHAT YOU NEED

- 2 avocados, pitted, peeled, and diced
  Juice of 1 lime
- 1 (15.5-ounce) can black beans
- 2 cups fresh or frozen corn
- 1 tomato, diced
- 1 red or green bell pepper, diced
- 3 garlic cloves, crushed
- 2 tablespoons chopped fresh cilantro
- 1 teaspoon ground cumin
- 1 teaspoon salt
- ¼ teaspoon ground black pepper

HERE'S WHAT YOU DO

1

Put the diced avocados in a large bowl, and pour the lime juice over them. Toss gently to coat.

2

Open the can of black beans. Rinse and drain the beans in a colander set in the sink. Add them to the bowl with the avocados.

3

Add the corn, tomato, bell pepper, garlic, cilantro, cumin, salt, and pepper.

4

Stir well. Chill until ready to eat!

HOW TO . . .

CUT UP AN AVOCADO

Avocados add flavor and a creamy texture to this tasty salad. You can often find ripe avocados on sale.

1 Start with a ripe avocado. It should feel soft but not mushy. Cut the avocado in half with a sharp knife, cutting around the hard pit in the middle.

2 Twist the cut avocado into two halves.

3 Pop out the pit with a spoon.

4 Hold one avocado half in the palm of your hand. Using a butter knife, cut lines along the length of the avocado.

5 Then cut lines across the width of the avocado, making cubes.

6 Use a spoon to scoop out the diced avocado pieces into a bowl.

Terrific Tabbouleh

MAKES 4 TO 6 SERVINGS

This **Middle Eastern salad** is made of finely chopped parsley, tomatoes, and mint, and bulgur, which is made from cracked wheat. Serve it as a side dish or **spoon it into a pita pocket** for a healthy dinner sandwich.

HERE'S WHAT YOU NEED

- 1 cup bulgur (medium grind)
- 2 cups hot water
- ¼ cup lemon juice (about 1 lemon)
- ¼ cup olive oil
- 1 teaspoon salt
- 1 garlic clove, crushed (optional)
- 2 tomatoes, cored, seeded, and diced
- 1 cucumber, seeded and diced
- 1 cup peas (optional)
- 1 cup chickpeas (optional)
- 1 cup chopped fresh parsley (about 1 bunch)
- ½ cup chopped fresh mint

HERE'S WHAT YOU DO

1 Put the bulgur in a large bowl. Pour in the hot water. Cover the bowl and let the bulgur sit until it is soft, about 45 minutes.

4 Add the tomatoes and cucumber to the bowl. You can also add peas and/or chickpeas, if you'd like.

2

Place a strainer in the sink. Pour in the bulgur and water. Press to remove the liquid. Return the bulgur to the bowl.

3

Stir in the lemon juice, oil, salt, and garlic, if using.

5

Add the parsley and mint. Stir up the tabbouleh. Give it a taste. Add extra salt, if you'd like.

6

Cover and refrigerate for at least 1 hour and up to 2 days.

HOW TO . . .

MAKE PITA CHIPS

These crispy snacks are a cinch to make—and they're the perfect scoop for Terrific Tabbouleh.

1 Preheat the broiler on your oven.

2 Cut open 2 pita pockets with kitchen scissors. Place the pitas, one at a time, on a cutting board. Using a pizza wheel, cut them into eight triangles. Lightly oil a baking sheet. Arrange the triangles in a single layer on the baking sheet.

3 Mix ¼ cup olive oil, 1 crushed garlic clove, and ½ teaspoon salt in a shallow bowl. Using a pastry brush (or just your clean fingers!), paint the pita triangles evenly with the oil mixture.

4 Broil the pita chips for a minute or two, until they are light brown and crispy. Watch closely because they burn fast!

Pasta with Tomatoes, Basil & Fresh Mozzarella

MAKES 4 SERVINGS

If you're craving pasta for dinner, try serving it with this **easy, no-cook pasta sauce**. This recipe calls for bow-tie pasta, but you can **use any fun shape** you like.

HERE'S WHAT YOU NEED

- ½ pound fresh mozzarella
  Small bunch of fresh basil
- ¼ cup olive oil
- 2 large ripe tomatoes, chopped
- 1 garlic clove, crushed
- 1 teaspoon salt
- 1 (1-pound) box bow-tie or other pasta
  Freshly grated Parmesan cheese, for serving

HERE'S WHAT YOU DO

1 Cut the mozzarella into bite-size pieces, and place in a large serving bowl.

2 Snip the basil leaves with clean scissors, and measure about ⅓ cup into the bowl.

3 Add the olive oil, tomatoes, garlic, and salt to the bowl. Stir well, then taste, and add more salt if you like. Set aside to let the flavors blend together while you cook the pasta.

4 Cook the pasta. Drain the noodles, then toss the warm noodles with the mozzarella and tomatoes.

5 Serve on plates, and garnish with any remaining basil, if you like. Pass the Parmesan cheese, please!

TIP Reserve 1 cup of water from the pasta cooking pot before you drain the pasta. That way, if your pasta gets sticky or your sauce needs thinning, you can add a little bit of pasta water without diluting the flavor.

HOW TO . . .
COOK PASTA

1 Fill a large pot with water. (The pot has to be large so that the pasta has plenty of room to cook and doesn't stick together.)

Bring to a boil over high heat. When the water begins to boil, add 1 teaspoon salt.

2 Carefully add the pasta. Let the water come back to a boil, and then lower the heat to medium-high.

Stir frequently during the first few minutes and occasionally at the end.

3 Set a timer. Look on the box for the recommended cooking time for the type of pasta you are cooking.

When the timer goes off, use a slotted spoon or tongs to carefully pull out a piece of pasta. Taste it. If you like the texture, drain the pasta.

4 To do this, set a colander in the sink, carefully carry the pot over to the sink, and pour the contents of the pot into the colander. (Practice doing this with adult supervision, as carrying hot water can be dangerous.)

Toss the drained pasta in your sauce immediately and serve.

Nutty Noodles

MAKES 4 TO 6 SERVINGS

Make these **tasty restaurant-style noodles** at home with this easy recipe. You can buy Chinese noodles in the refrigerator section of most grocery stores, or use any kind of long, thin noodles like spaghetti.

HERE'S WHAT YOU NEED

- 1 pound lo mein noodles
- ¼ cup creamy peanut butter
- ½ cup warm water
- ¼ cup soy sauce
- 1 tablespoon chopped fresh ginger
- 1 garlic clove, crushed
  Toppings of your choice

HERE'S WHAT YOU DO

1

Cook the noodles according to the package directions. Drain and rinse with cold water.

2

In a large bowl, use a fork or whisk to stir the peanut butter with the warm water until it is creamy.

3

Stir in the soy sauce, ginger, and garlic.

4

Add the noodles to the bowl. Toss well and serve with toppings on the side (see Nutty Noodle Toppings).

NUTTY NOODLE TOPPINGS

- Grated carrot
- Scallions (sliced into rounds)
- Cucumber (peeled, seeded, and thinly sliced)
- Chopped roasted peanuts
- Toasted sesame seeds
- Steamed edamame
- Steamed broccoli florets
- Freshly squeezed lime juice
- Thinly sliced green or red bell peppers

Black Beans & Rice

MAKES 4 SERVINGS

This nutritious dish is **easy to make and delicious**. Serve it with a squeeze of lime and tortilla chips on the side. You can also *jazz it up* with **salsa** and **shredded cheese**.

HERE'S WHAT YOU NEED

- 1 tablespoon olive oil
- 1 small onion, diced
- 1 green bell pepper, diced
- 3 garlic cloves, crushed
- 1 teaspoon sugar
- ½ teaspoon dried oregano
- 1 (15.5-ounce) can black beans
- 1 cup white rice
- Lime wedges (optional)

HERE'S WHAT YOU DO

1 Heat the oil in a large pot over medium-low heat. Add the onion and pepper. Sauté until soft, about 5 minutes.

2 Stir in the garlic, sugar, and oregano.

3 Pour the liquid from the beans can into a 2-cup measuring cup. Add enough water so the liquid measures 2 cups.

4 Pour the liquid into the pot. Stir in the beans and rice.

5 Turn up the heat and bring the rice and beans to a boil. Then reduce the heat to low. Simmer, covered, until the rice absorbs all the water, about 25 minutes.

6 To serve, spoon onto a plate or shallow bowl. If you'd like, you can also serve with a squeeze of lime.

Fried Rice

MAKES 4 SERVINGS

If you have cooked rice left over from another dinner, turn it into tonight's dinner with this recipe for a **Chinese restaurant favorite**. Make sure to **use cold rice** instead of warm rice so that the finished dish is not mushy.

HERE'S WHAT YOU NEED

- 3 large eggs
- 2 tablespoons vegetable oil
- ½ teaspoon toasted sesame oil
- 4 scallions, sliced
- 1 cup frozen peas
- 1 medium carrot, grated
- 1 tablespoon grated ginger
- 1 garlic clove, crushed
- 3 cups cooked and chilled white rice
- 1½–2 tablespoons soy sauce

HOW TO . . .
COOK RICE

Cooked just right, plain rice makes a tasty, healthy side dish. It can also be the basis for all kinds of meals because it mixes well with so many different ingredients and sauces.

Here's how to cook it. Depending on which kind of rice you make, 1 cup uncooked rice will make 3 to 4 cups when cooked.

Bring 2 cups water to a boil. Add 1 cup rice, stir, cover, and reduce the heat to low. Simmer for 15 to 20 minutes, until all the water is absorbed. (Brown rice takes 30 to 35 minutes to cook.)

HERE'S WHAT YOU DO

1

Break the eggs into a small bowl. Beat them with a fork or small whisk.

2

Heat 1½ tablespoons of the vegetable oil and all of the sesame oil in a large wok or skillet over medium heat.

3

Slowly and carefully (to avoid being splattered by hot oil!) add the scallions, peas, carrot, ginger, and garlic. Sauté the vegetables for a minute, stirring constantly.

4

Add the rice and heat for 2 to 3 minutes, stirring occasionally.

5

Push the rice to the edges of the pan, and pour the remaining ½ tablespoon vegetable oil into the center. Add the eggs and stir until they are cooked and scrambled.

6

Stir the eggs into the rice until everything is mixed up. Add the soy sauce and heat for another minute or two, stirring often. Serve with additional soy sauce.

Luscious Lentils & Rice

MAKES 4 TO 6 SERVINGS

For **yummy comfort food** that's **packed with protein**, cook up some of this lentil and rice mixture. You can buy both the lentils and rice in the bulk dried-food section of your grocery store.

HERE'S WHAT YOU NEED

1 cup dried brown lentils
4 cups chicken or vegetable broth
2 cups water
1 cup white rice
3 tablespoons olive oil
1 large onion, chopped
   Salt and ground black pepper

OPTIONAL TOPPINGS
   Chopped parsley
   Chopped tomato
   Diced cucumber
   Plain yogurt

HERE'S WHAT YOU DO

1

Rinse the lentils in a strainer and pick out any stones. Transfer the lentils to a soup pot, and pour in the broth and water. Cook uncovered over medium heat for 30 minutes.

2

Reduce the heat to low and stir in the rice. Cover the pot and cook until the rice and lentils have absorbed all the liquid, about 20 minutes.

3

If the rice and lentils are still crunchy but the liquid is all gone after 20 minutes, add another 1 cup water and cook for 10 minutes longer.

4

While the lentils and rice cook, heat the oil in a skillet over medium heat. Add the onion and sauté until soft, about 5 minutes.

5

Add salt and pepper to the hot lentils and rice, tasting as you go, until you like the flavor. Scoop the mixture into bowls. Top with the cooked onions.

6

Add any of the toppings you like.

Pizza Night!

MAKES 2 LARGE PIZZAS

Turn your kitchen into a **pizza factory** with this easy, made-from-scratch dough. It's fun to let your family **customize their own pizzas** (or part of a pizza) with their favorite toppings.

HERE'S WHAT YOU NEED

DOUGH

- 1 tablespoon (1 packet) active dry yeast
- 2 teaspoons sugar
- 2½ cups warm water (it should feel like bathwater)
- 6 cups flour
- 2 tablespoons olive oil, plus 1 tablespoon for oiling the bowl
- 2½ teaspoons salt

PIZZA

- 2 cups pizza sauce
- 8 ounces shredded mozzarella cheese
- Toppings: olives, green peppers, pepperoni, mushrooms, or whatever you like

At step 6, preheat the oven to 400°F (200°C).

1

Mix the yeast and sugar in a large bowl. Add the warm water and whisk until the yeast and sugar are dissolved.

5

Punch the dough down. Divide it in half, one for each pizza.

2

Add the flour, 2 tablespoons of the oil, and the salt, and stir until you can make a soft ball of the dough. Turn the dough out onto a lightly floured countertop.

3

Dust your hands with flour and knead the dough until it is smooth and elastic, about 5 minutes. Rub the inside of a clean bowl with the remaining 1 tablespoon olive oil.

4

Place the dough in the bowl, and turn to coat it with the oil. Cover with plastic wrap and let it rise for about 30 minutes.

6

Preheat the oven to 400°F (200°C). Lightly oil two baking sheets. Stretch out the dough onto the oiled sheets. If the dough is too hard to flatten out, let it rest for 10 minutes and then try again.

7

Top each pizza with pizza sauce, shredded cheese, and the toppings of your choice.

8

Bake for 15 to 20 minutes, or until the cheese is bubbly and the crust is golden brown.

Breakfast for Dinner Pancakes

MAKES 4 TO 6 SERVINGS

Switch up dinner by **making breakfast at night**. Serve these yummy pancakes with other breakfast favorites like orange juice and bacon. And **eat dinner in your pjs** for extra fun!

HERE'S WHAT YOU NEED

- 1 cup all-purpose flour
- 2 tablespoons sugar
- 2 teaspoons baking powder
  Pinch of salt
- 2 eggs
- ¾ cup milk
- 2 tablespoons butter, melted, plus more butter for the pan
  Maple syrup, for serving

HOW TO . . .
BOIL AN EGG

Eggs are a good way to add some protein to your diet, whether you're eating pancakes for dinner or looking for an easy lunch or snack.

Place 4 eggs in a small saucepan and cover with cold water. **Bring** the water to a boil over high heat. **Boil** the eggs for 1 minute, then turn off the heat. **Put** the lid on the saucepan, and let the eggs sit in the hot water for 10 minutes. **Pour** off the hot water, and run cold water into the pan to cool off the eggs.

Roll the eggs gently on a countertop or cutting board to crack the shells, then peel them. If it's hard to peel off the shells, try holding the eggs under running water while you peel them.

HERE'S WHAT YOU DO

1 Mix the flour, sugar, baking powder, and salt in a large bowl.

2 In another bowl, whisk the eggs. Then stir in the milk and melted butter.

3 Pour the egg mixture over the flour mixture and stir until mixed. It's okay to have a few lumps in the batter. If you mix it too much, your pancakes might turn out a little chewy.

4 Heat a griddle or frying pan over medium-high heat. Melt a small pat of butter in the pan, and spread it around with a spatula. Fill a ¼-cup measuring cup with pancake batter, and ladle it onto the griddle.

5 Repeat until the griddle is full, leaving a few inches between each pancake. Cook the pancakes until the edges are dry and bubbles appear on the surface, about 2 minutes.

6 Then flip the pancakes and cook the second side. Serve the pancakes warm with maple syrup.

Ramen Noodle Soup

MAKES 2 SERVINGS

Ramen noodle soup is a **quick, inexpensive, and filling meal**, but the kind you buy in the store is loaded with salt and preservatives—and not as good as homemade! You can buy plain noodles and jazz them up with your own ingredients for a **healthy version that tastes better** than the packaged one.

EXTRA FLAVOR

Stir any of these into your ramen noodle soup, tasting as you go. A little goes a long way with most of these!

- Mirin (rice wine)
- Miso paste
- Sesame oil
- Soy sauce
- Hard-boiled egg
- Nori (seaweed)
- Bean sprouts

HERE'S WHAT YOU NEED

1	tablespoon sesame or vegetable oil
2–4	garlic cloves, crushed
1–2	tablespoons grated ginger
4	cups miso or chicken broth
2	cups water
1	tablespoon soy sauce
6–10	shiitake mushrooms, thinly sliced (optional)
1	carrot, cut into rounds
¾	cup diced firm tofu or cooked shrimp, beef, or chicken
2	(3-ounce) packages ramen or other Asian noodles
2	scallions, chopped

HERE'S WHAT YOU DO

1

Heat the oil in a medium pot over medium heat. Add the garlic and ginger, and cook for about 3 minutes.

2

Pour the broth and water into the pot. Add the soy sauce and turn up the heat to high.

3

Add the mushrooms, carrot, and tofu, and cook for 5 minutes.

4

Add the noodles and let the soup cook for about 3 minutes, or until the noodles are soft.

5

Ladle the soup into bowls. Garnish with the scallions and any of the suggested stir-ins for extra flavor.

Shakshuka

MAKES 4 SERVINGS

One of the best things about this classic stew is that you **can eat it any time** of day—for breakfast, lunch, or dinner! Serve it with a loaf of hearty bread for sopping up the **yummy tomato sauce**.

HERE'S WHAT YOU NEED

- 3 tablespoons olive oil
- 1 small yellow onion, chopped
- 1 large red bell pepper, chopped
- 2 garlic cloves, crushed
- 2 teaspoons ground smoked paprika
- 1¼ teaspoons ground cumin
- 1 teaspoon salt
- ½ teaspoon ground black pepper
- 1 (28-ounce) can chopped tomatoes
- 4 eggs
- ¼ cup crumbled feta cheese
- ¼ cup chopped fresh parsley
  Bread, for serving

Preheat the oven to 375°F (190°C).

HERE'S WHAT YOU DO

1

Warm the oil in a large cast-iron or ovenproof skillet over medium heat. Add the onion and bell pepper, and cook until they begin to brown, about 5 minutes.

2

Reduce the heat to medium-low. Continue to cook, stirring occasionally, until the onion and pepper are soft, about 3 minutes longer.

3

Stir in the garlic and cook for 1 minute. Add the paprika, cumin, salt, and black pepper, and cook until fragrant, about 1 minute.

4

Add the tomatoes and cook, stirring occasionally, until the sauce thickens, about 10 minutes. Remove from the heat. Make four small wells and crack an egg into each.

5

Place the pan in the oven. Bake for about 10 minutes, until the egg whites are set (for a firm yolk, bake for 2 to 3 minutes longer).

6

Remove the pan from the oven carefully. Top the dish with the feta and parsley. Serve immediately, with bread.

Popcorn Chicken

MAKES 4 SERVINGS

Don't chicken out! It's easy to serve up your own **crunchy chicken bites** for dinner. Cut the chicken into bite-size chunks for Popcorn Chicken and **dunk them into different sauces**.

PICK A SAUCE

Serve your chicken bites with one of these tasty mixtures.

HONEY-MUSTARD SAUCE

Mix together ½ cup mustard with 1 to 2 tablespoons honey.

BUFFALO SAUCE

Whisk 3 tablespoons melted butter with 1 teaspoon ground cayenne pepper. Mix in 2 teaspoons white vinegar and a pinch of salt.

CURRY MAYO

Mix ½ cup mayonnaise with 1 tablespoon curry powder and 1 to 2 teaspoons milk until creamy.

TIP You can also use these dips with veggies!

HERE'S WHAT YOU DO

1

Put the chicken pieces in a bowl. Mix up the egg, milk, salt, and pepper in another bowl. Pour the breadcrumbs into a third bowl.

2

Line up the three bowls. Dip each piece of chicken first into the egg wash, then into the breadcrumbs.

3

When all the pieces are coated, heat the olive oil in a large skillet over medium-high heat.

4

Add the chicken and cook until golden, about 3 minutes on each side.

5

Transfer the cooked chicken to a serving plate. Set out a variety of dipping sauces and dive in!

Chicken Curry

MAKES 4 SERVINGS

Curry powder is the secret to this **flavorful chicken dish**. Many spices are in curry powder—cardamom, turmeric, cumin, coriander, cloves, and more. You can buy lots of different kinds of **prepared curry powder** at the grocery store.

HERE'S WHAT YOU NEED

1 tablespoon vegetable oil
1 small onion, chopped
1 garlic clove, crushed
1 tablespoon curry powder
½ teaspoon salt
1 pound boneless, skinless chicken thighs or breasts, cut into 2-inch chunks
1 cup coconut milk
Hot cooked rice, for serving

HERE'S WHAT YOU DO

1

Heat the oil in a large skillet over medium-high heat. Add the onion and garlic, and sauté for 5 minutes.

2

Stir in the curry powder and salt.

3

Add the chicken and sauté until the outside is golden brown, about 5 minutes.

4

Pour the coconut milk over the chicken.

5

Bring the coconut milk to a boil, then reduce the heat to low.

6

Simmer, uncovered, stirring occasionally, until the chicken is cooked through, about 10 minutes. Serve hot over cooked rice.

Chicken Satay

MAKES 4 SERVINGS

Grilled chicken skewers served with a peanut-coconut sauce are a restaurant favorite. Try making them at home with this recipe. Serve them with **extra peanut sauce** for dipping.

HERE'S WHAT YOU NEED

- 2 pounds boneless, skinless chicken thighs, cut into 1-inch chunks
- ½ cup peanut butter
- 1 cup coconut milk
- 1 tablespoon soy sauce
- 1 tablespoon lime juice
- 1 teaspoon mild curry powder
- 1 garlic clove, crushed
  Hot cooked rice, for serving (optional)

OPTIONAL TOPPINGS
- Cucumber strips
- Crushed peanuts
- Lime wedges
- Chopped cilantro

Preheat the oven to 400°F (200°C).

HERE'S WHAT YOU DO

1

Thread the chicken pieces onto metal skewers, and set on a tray or plate.

2

Combine the peanut butter, coconut milk, soy sauce, lime juice, curry powder, and garlic in a saucepan.

3

Cook over medium-low heat, whisking until the sauce is creamy and thick. Turn off the heat and let the sauce cool.

4

Spoon half of the cooled sauce over the chicken, coating all the pieces.

5

Bake the skewers for 15 to 20 minutes, turning once, until the chicken pieces are evenly cooked and light brown on each side.

6

Warm the remaining sauce over low heat. Pour the sauce into a bowl for dipping. You can also serve the skewers with rice and optional toppings.

Beef Empanadas

MAKES 10 EMPANADAS

These **tasty pocket pastries** are fun to make and eat. **Add green olives and hard-boiled eggs** to the spicy ground beef filling for extra flavor. You can buy empanada wrappers in the international freezer section of most grocery stores.

HERE'S WHAT YOU NEED

FILLING

- 1 tablespoon vegetable oil, plus extra to grease the baking sheet
- 1 small white onion, diced (about ½ cup)
- 2 teaspoons chili powder
- 1 teaspoon ground cumin
- 1 teaspoon garlic powder
- 1 teaspoon dried oregano
- ½ teaspoon salt
- 1 pound ground beef

EMPANADAS

- 10 empanada wrappers, defrosted if frozen
- 2 hard-boiled eggs, sliced (optional)
- ½ cup sliced green olives (optional)
- 1 egg (for the egg wash)

Preheat the oven to 375°F (190°C).

DIPPING SAUCES

Serve your empanadas nice and warm with any of these dipping sauces.

- Tomato sauce
- Salsa
- Ketchup

HERE'S WHAT YOU DO

1

Heat 1 tablespoon oil in a skillet over medium heat. Add the onions. Sauté until the onions are soft, about 5 minutes. Then stir in the chili powder, cumin, garlic powder, oregano, and salt.

2

Add the ground beef. Break up the meat into small pieces with a spatula. Stir and cook until the meat is brown, about 8 minutes. Turn off the heat and let the mixture cool.

3

Place an empanada wrapper on a cutting board. Spoon a tablespoon or two of the filling into the center of the wrapper. Add a few slices of hard-boiled egg and/or green olives, if you'd like.

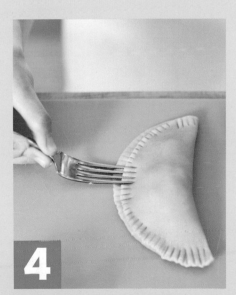

4

Fold the wrapper in half. Press the edges gently with the tines of a fork to seal the filling inside. (If the dough doesn't stick, rub a few drops of water on the inside edges before sealing.) Fill the remaining wrappers.

5

Grease a baking sheet with oil. Whisk the egg in a small bowl. Transfer the finished empanadas to the oiled baking sheet. Brush the egg onto each empanada with a pastry brush.

6

Bake for 20 minutes, or until golden on top.

Meatballs with Creamy Sauce

MAKES ABOUT 40 MEATBALLS

These **mini meatballs** make a full meal with this **tasty cream sauce**. If you don't want to make the sauce, you can serve the meatballs with pasta sauce instead. Or serve them as a finger food with one of the dipping sauces shown on page 48 and some veggies on the side.

dipping sauces shown on page 48

HERE'S WHAT YOU NEED

MEATBALLS
- ½ cup breadcrumbs
- ¼ cup milk
- 1 pound ground beef
- 1 pound ground pork
- 1 egg, beaten
- 1 teaspoon salt
- ¼ teaspoon ground black pepper

CREAMY SAUCE
- 1 cup beef stock
- 1 cup heavy cream
- 3 tablespoons flour
- 1 tablespoon soy sauce

Cooked noodles, for serving (optional)

Preheat the oven to 400°F (200°C).

HERE'S WHAT YOU DO

1

Mix the breadcrumbs and milk in a small bowl, and let soak for a few minutes.

2

Place the ground beef and pork in a large bowl. Add the egg, salt, pepper, and breadcrumbs. Mix with a large spoon (or clean hands).

3

Shape the mixture into 1-inch meatballs, and place the balls on an ungreased baking sheet.

4

Bake for 15 minutes, or until the meatballs are cooked through and no longer pink in the middle.

5

Meanwhile, whisk the beef stock, cream, flour, and soy sauce in a large saucepan. Cook over low heat, stirring, until the sauce is creamy and thick, about 10 minutes.

6

Add the meatballs to the pan, and coat them in the sauce. Cook until the meatballs are hot. Serve over noodles, if you like.

Super Sliders

MAKES 4 SERVINGS

Mix up **a batch of mini burgers**—also known as sliders—with a few easy ingredients. Bake them on a sheet pan in the oven. Serve them on dinner rolls, add toppings, and **pass the ketchup**!

HERE'S WHAT YOU NEED

- 1½ pounds ground beef
- 1 egg
- ⅓ cup breadcrumbs
- 1 garlic clove, crushed
- 2 teaspoons dried oregano
- 1 teaspoon salt
- 8 small slices of your favorite cheese (optional)
- 8 dinner rolls
  Toppings (whatever you like), for serving

Preheat the oven to 350°F (150°C).

SLIDER TOPPINGS

- Ketchup
- Mayonnaise
- Mustard
- Relish
- Bacon
- Chopped onion
- Pickles
- Lettuce
- Tomato slices

HERE'S WHAT YOU DO

1

Put the ground beef, egg, bread-crumbs, garlic, oregano, and salt in a large bowl.

2

Mix everything together with your (clean!) hands or a wooden spoon.

3

Shape the meat mixture into 8 patties. Wash your hands again!

4

Place the burgers on a sheet pan. Bake for 20 minutes, turning once after 10 minutes.

5

To make cheeseburgers, if you like, top each one with a quarter slice of cheese when the burgers are just a minute or two away from being done. Let the cheese melt while the burgers finish cooking.

6

Cut the dinner rolls in half and place a burger on the bottom half of each one. Put the burgers on a serving platter.

Think Spring Rolls

MAKES 6 TO 8 SERVINGS

For a **no-cook dinner on a hot night**, try this Vietnamese favorite. Fill rice-paper wrappers with lettuce, grated carrot, and fresh herbs. (You can buy spring roll wrappers in most grocery stores.) **Roll them up**, step back, and watch them disappear!

HERE'S WHAT YOU NEED

- 1 head Boston lettuce, chopped
- 2 carrots, grated
- 10 sprigs fresh mint, finely chopped
- 10 sprigs fresh cilantro, finely chopped
- 1 cup cooked chopped shrimp, chicken, or pork or cubed tofu (optional)
- 12 spring roll wrappers
- 2–3 tablespoons hoisin sauce
- ¼–½ cup chopped peanuts (optional) Dipping sauce, for serving (see recipe below)

DIPPING SAUCE
MAKES ABOUT ¾ CUP

HERE'S WHAT YOU NEED

- ¼ cup smooth peanut butter
- ¼ cup hot water
- 2 tablespoons soy sauce
- 2 tablespoons honey
- 2 tablespoons lime juice

HERE'S WHAT YOU DO

Whisk together the peanut butter and hot water in a small bowl until smooth. Add the soy sauce, honey, and lime juice and whisk again.

HERE'S WHAT YOU DO

1 Lay out the lettuce, carrots, mint, cilantro, and shrimp or other protein, if you're using it, on a large plate or cutting board.

2 Fill a pie plate with warm tap water. Soak one spring roll wrapper in the warm water until it is soft, about 30 seconds.

3 Lay the softened wrapper on a cutting board. Working with rice paper is a little tricky (and sticky!) at first, but you'll get the hang of it. It's cool to see the crisp wafers transform into slippery wrappers!

4 To assemble a roll, top the wrapper with the lettuce, carrots, mint, cilantro, and shrimp or other protein, if you're using it. Drizzle with a teaspoonful or so of hoisin sauce, and sprinkle with some peanuts, if you like.

5 Fold the sides in and roll the wrapper up around the filling, as shown. Set it aside and repeat soaking and filling the wrappers until you've used up all the wrappers and filling. Cut the spring rolls in half. Serve with the dipping sauce.

Fantastic Fish Tacos

MAKES 8 TO 10 TACOS

This **Tex-Mex favorite** starts with a rub—a simple spice mix that you spread on the fish before you cook it. You can also spread the rub on steak or chicken. Once the fish is cooked, wrap it up in **warm corn tortillas** and add your favorite toppings.

HERE'S WHAT YOU NEED

- 1 tablespoon chili powder
- 1 tablespoon ground cumin
- ½ teaspoon salt
- 1 pound haddock or other firm white fish
- 2 tablespoons vegetable oil
- 8-10 corn tortillas
- Toppings of your choice

Preheat the oven to 300°F (150°C).

TACO TOPPING BAR

These toppings make delicious additions to your fish tacos. Choose any combo you like!

Shredded cabbage	Salsa	Guacamole
Grated Monterey Jack cheese	Corn & Black Bean Salad (page 26)	

Chili-lime cream: In a small bowl, stir together ½ cup sour cream, 2 teaspoons freshly squeezed lime juice, ½ crushed garlic clove, ½ teaspoon chili powder, and salt to taste.

HERE'S WHAT YOU DO

1

Mix the chili powder, cumin, and salt on a large plate. Carefully press the fish into the spice mixture to coat it on both sides.

2

Heat the oil in a large skillet over medium-high heat. Add the fish and cook on both sides until white in the center. The time will vary depending on the thickness of the fish, but it should be 2 to 3 minutes per side.

3

Remove the fish from the skillet, and place on a serving plate. Let it cool slightly, then gently pull it apart into shreds or chunks with a fork.

4

Wrap the tortillas in aluminum foil, and warm them in the oven for about 10 minutes.

5

Set out a variety of toppings (see the list of ideas on the opposite page), and let everyone create their own taco combinations.

Weeknight Meal Planning and Shopping List

Use this chart to plan your meals and figure out the ingredients you need to buy. You can find a downloadable version at https://www.storey.com/kids-cook-dinner-list.

Menu	Shopping List
Monday	
Tuesday	
Wednesday	
Thursday	
Friday	